BEAUTIFUL BROKENNESS:

Redefine Your Beauty by Breaking Through Emotional Roadblocks, Elevating Your Mind with a Renewed Mindset, and Evolving in God's Divine Purpose

SHAKELA T. MATTHEWS

Table of Contents

Preface

Do you have a hard time looking in the mirror? Because you see the hurt, pain, failures, and brokenness. It's time to uncover your beauty by breaking up with your fears, awakening your potential, and walking in your purpose! What is your biggest fear about your marriage ending? Friend, are you letting the prospect of divorce ruin your self-image? Are you prepared for the financial stresses divorce may bring? I decree and declare that you will no longer live in your past because your mistakes do not define who you are. No matter what you've experienced, you can use it to grow. Pick up those broken pieces, revolutionize your life, and know that God uses broken things to produce greatness. It takes broken soil to produce a crop, broken clouds to give rain, broken grain to give bread, broken bread to give strength…Peter, weeping bitterly, returns to greater power than ever. ~ Vance Havner

Introduction

"You are more BEAUTIFUL because you've been BROKEN!"

Welcome to BEAUTIFUL BROKENNESS: Redefine Your Beauty by Breaking Through Emotional Roadblocks, Elevating Your Mind with a Renewed Mindset, and Evolving in God's Divine Purpose. I want to personally thank you for purchasing my book. My hope is that by the time you reach the end of this book, you will have the knowledge and tools to cope with your raw emotions, rebuild after your divorce, reclaim your confidence, and be empowered to walk into your God-given purpose successfully and gracefully.

Marriage can be wonderful, and it takes work from both parties. But it can also become incredibly complex when the two no longer see eye to eye. Sadly, for many of us, our fairy tale marriage ends in divorce despite our best efforts (at which point, we are forced to make a decision that frightens us because of the unknowns in our financial status, reactions from our children, emotions, and the thought of starting over). You could be like me, afraid to make the best decision for yourself because of how you think people would perceive you.

Going through a divorce can also trick your mind into thinking that you no longer have a purpose because you are so consumed with the thoughts of betrayal, rage, doubt, fear, hurt, and embarrassment, which are all signs of unforgiveness. Do you feel like you will never recover from the hurt, betrayal, or unforgiveness? If so, it is time for you to change your story. Unforgiveness turns your heart cold and keeps you from completely healing and, in turn, affects your breakthrough and your ability to flourish in your purpose. Sis, let me remind you that your life is full of purpose no matter the situation or struggles that you have endured. You have the ability to reclaim what is yours, free from pain, shame, regret, fear, anger, and depression. Instead of focusing on the hurt, use it to empower you to become stronger.

I have successfully overcome two divorces despite the challenges they both presented. I gained wisdom through personal experiences of heartbreak and deep emotional wounds on my journey towards healing, loving myself, reclaiming my worth, loving others, and discovering my purpose. God gave me light in my darkest season, and I can now let it shine like a diamond. A twice-divorced mother of two small children at the time left me so broken. Those experiences made me feel like a failure not only as a wife and mother but also as a woman. I did not know how to cope with the emotions, and I felt trapped and quickly sinking, although I wore a perfect smile. I no longer thought I was worthy of love or experiencing a serious relationship. I made many decisions that went against my upbringing and character, and I knew I needed change. By the grace of God and the implementation of the strategies that I have introduced in this book, I was able to break through emotional barriers, overcome financial bondage, learn the power of forgiveness, and pick up the shattered pieces of what was once broken and transform into a beautiful woman God has called me to be.

My turning point was when my aunt came to me one day and said, "If you do not make some changes now, you will not be around to experience your parent's legacy."

WOW, talking about a wake-up call. I was awakened to the fact that I am a child of God, so I had nothing to fear concerning people's judgment. I realized that I was NOT condemned by my past, and NEITHER ARE YOU. Beautiful, you may have found yourself in a marriage where you have experienced infidelity, betrayal, abuse, or emotional turmoil and felt incomplete and seeking validation because you have lost sight of who you are. Maybe you can relate because you are divorced or contemplating divorce because you are spiritually, mentally, and emotionally broken. You might be searching for your purpose or trying to navigate steps while coping with your emotions. Be encouraged and know you can break through those emotional barriers of lingering anger and deep wounds. Sometimes we experience breaking points and stay broken, but we must change our viewpoint and allow the breaking to transform into your blessing. Your hardest struggles, deepest wounds, and greatest fears are among the most beautiful precious, and admirable parts of you.

The overall purpose of this book is to help you become intentional about receiving your breakthrough by learning how to deal with those raw emotions and forgiveness, reclaim your self-worth, rediscover your purpose, and revitalize your life by awakening to your greatness. If you do not learn how to forgive, it will keep you from completely healing. Without completely healing, you will stay stuck and continue to be a victim. The danger of being stuck is that you cannot move forward and jeopardize missing where God wants to take you. Procrastination in coping with your emotions and learning how to deal with them healthily delays you in reclaiming your life and discovering your purpose.

Jesus sees us at our worst, in our brokenness and pain, and guess what? He still chose to give us purpose because what once was broken was made whole and beautiful. This book is a practical guide for healing with the necessary steps to help you intentionally excavate your thoughts and cope with your emotions and fears that may prevent you from thriving and walking into your purpose. Lord, we offer our broken pieces as an offering to you. Thank you for mending the pieces for everyone reading this book and making them whole again so they can walk in the beautiful purpose you have ordained for their lives.

Your new life and purpose are awaiting you. Let's claim it because you have the power to redefine your own beauty!

~ Signed ~

Kela T Matthews

Chapter 1

Mosaic Decision

All things work together for the good of those who love God: and are called according to his purpose.

Romans 8:28

Many can attest that when it comes to decision-making, we can find ourselves going in a direction that we never planned or fully thought out. If we are honest with ourselves, we inherently know, based on biases, reasons, emotions, and memories, that it may not be the best decision for us to make at the moment. Experience has taught us that relying on God's power and guidance frees us from prematurely making dangerous and life-altering decisions.

As a child, like many, the idea of marriage excited/fascinated me, and as an experienced adult, I realized that I fell in love with the idea without knowing what marriage really was. I declared to anyone who would listen, even myself, that I would be married with kids by the age of twenty-five because of family and societal programming. Friend, if you are forty, still unmarried, and have no kids, you are perfect right where you are! Keep walking in your design and purpose! Things were so much different in past generations than they are now, and back in the day, twenty-five was considered old, but today we realize you are just starting to live. I remember my elders saying that by that age, you needed to start your family because you needed to be done having children at the age of thirty. Whew, chile, why did I ever listen to that advice? I should have learned how to talk and, more importantly, listen to God a little more back then because it would have saved me from some things, hunny. Nowadays, we are so much more educated; I could not begin to imagine my eldest son, who is only twenty years of age, coming to me saying he is ready to get married or, better yet, have a child.

Friend - I feel like I can call you all my friends since I am now spilling all my tea to you – in 2002, at the age of twenty-five, after the birth of my first child, I was married to my first husband. You could not tell me anything because I thought all my dreams had come true, and I was walking on cloud nine. Not realizing this marriage would cause me to lose sight of myself by accepting actions and treatment that constantly required me to dishonor myself. Not realizing that I would experience a child being born within my marriage that I did not birth or realizing that what I thought were truths were only lies. The thought of divorce devastated me, made me feel inadequate, and I lost my sense of self. It caused me to neglect the truth my inner self once knew; when I would have normally screamed, my inner self secretly whispered, LET IT GO to a lot of things. I was lost and remained in a shell, trying to do some soul-searching. By this time, I had two young children, and I was broken and lost.

Let's take a moment to define "Broken." Broken: having been fractured or damaged and no longer in one piece or working order; having given up all hope. How many of you know that broken crayons still color? Friends, they still have PURPOSE. I am unsure how many of you were like me, but I used to love to color and always preferred crayons over colored pencils. My crayons had to be sharp to outline what I was coloring and make it crisp, and when they would break or get dull, I would be so upset and throw them away, not realizing that they still had potential and a purpose. They could be repurposed or sharpened with a sharpener making them almost perfect again.

For many of us, when it comes to the decision to divorce our spouse, it can be a hard choice to make. We have shared our most intimate moments with this person and private conversations, and some may have felt like this person validated them. For some of us, it may not even be a decision that we have had to make but one that someone made for us, and we had to woman up and live with the results. Maybe it is not the decision you had hoped for, but you now have to plan to move forward.

A friend of mine, who was a young mother, married and dealing with a high-risk pregnancy when her husband of a few years came to her to tell her that he was filing for a divorce. Not to mention he was Deacon in the church spreading his goodies, as Ciara would say, all around. Can you imagine being pregnant with twins, on bed rest, underemployed, hypertensive, and unexpectedly facing divorce due to your spouse choosing to live a lifestyle totally opposite to the foundation your marriage was founded on? Then the unbelievable reality hits you straight in the face, the walls start to cave in, and you disappear into anger.

Let's all take a moment to breathe... because the thought of this can bring up a lot of emotions that we thought were in the past. "If you focus on the hurt, you will continue to suffer, but if you focus on the lesson, you will continue to grow," author unknown. I cannot tell you how many phone calls I have received over the years from friends and people who know little about me to ask how I accepted my decision to divorce.

Although I am happily married now and not in that place anymore, it was one of the hardest things I had to mentally endure while going through this process. I grew up as a "PK" (preacher's kid) within a Christian family, and divorce was not common. When I say a Christian family, I mean it. My parent, aunts, uncles, and grandparents were either pastors, bishops, evangelists, ministers, deacons, or had some role in the church. So, trying to talk to them was more like a prayer convention. Now, I needed the prayer, but I also really wanted advice. You know, a parent or listening ear versus a pastor in that moment. Come on now, you all know that back in the day, people stayed married no matter what, and now we have somewhat watered-down marriages. Our mothers and grandmothers were great examples of submission, as the bible says in Ephesians 5, for wives to submit themselves to their own husbands. I was initially scared of how people would perceive me and how my family would react to my decision. I just knew that I would be the talk of my family, and not in a good way. I felt like everyone would look down on me for a failed marriage.

Yes, I felt like a failure, and I beat myself up. I had the "maybe I could and should have done this" talks to myself. I thought about all the things that I could have done differently. I thought about the signs that I ignored. How many of you can agree that we are given signs? But we tend to look right past them just like a summer breeze blowing through our long silky pressed hair because we are in LOVE, and he has been whispering those sweet nothings in our ear. Not realizing that sometimes that breeze is a tornado waiting to happen. Now you are faced with a decision to make because of your family's biblical views on divorce.

Let us address these "Red Flags" before we continue. Reasons why we get into relationships even though we see the red flags: Many times, we are simply looking for validation. Some want to be chosen because of insecurities. Friends, be honest; we think we can change the person. We do not know what we truly want and tend to create illusions based on other people's relationships. Let me give you a few signs or "Red Flags" to look for. (Poor communication, shut down when having tough or emotional communications, avoiding responsibility, you cannot be yourself or having to change yourself, emotionally unavailable, gaslighting behavior, verbal and physical abuse, commitment issues, lack of respect.)

Now, back to the regularly scheduled program. I was stuck, and I saw no way out of my misery of making a decision that was deemed detrimental to my children and me until I realized that I was in a relationship that God had not ordained. I had all the signs not to enter, but I chose to ignore them. This decision was detrimental to me because I had so many concerns, like, will I ever have peace? How will I move forward? How will my decision affect my children? Am I giving up too soon, and is this the right decision? Will God be displeased with my decision? I felt like God was saying, I did not tell you to get into that situation in the first place. BOOM, there it was. I felt relieved and no longer cared what anyone thought about my decision. I looked in the mirror and said, Oh No, Girl, you are worth more than that.

Now, do not get me wrong because I am not perfect, and I'm not saying that my then spouse is a bad person. He just was not the person for me. I made my decision for ME. I began to take action and ensure that my children were ok, and I never looked back. You must trust that you will be ok and know when God has told you to walk away. I am not an advocate for divorce, but I realized that God does not intend for us to be in situations that cause us to go through hell.

We are our biggest critics and often, in self-examination, find ourselves putting more weight and barriers on our lives. This is the largest mistake we make because, in an attempt to shield ourselves from our self-reflection, we allow toxic people in our lives, including spouses who never should have been allowed access. Friends, an emotionally healthy woman does not need others to be her peace; she will not allow anyone to rob her of the gift of her PEACE. When you allow others to give you a piece of themselves, it will disrupt your peace!

The Naked Truth is in order to have a piece of something, it means that something is Broken! People say all the time you teach people how to treat you, and being accepting of poor behavior gives others permission to treat you less than you deserve. So, when you wonder why your mate is not spending adequate time investing in you and your relationship the way you desire, just look at what you have required.

Friends, lean in and take your power back. I employ you to stop accepting what is beneath your design for trying not to be the single one in the room. If you can't date and pour into yourself, how will you ever attract the one God ordained for you? Know your worth and add tax! Know who you are and whose you are!

Today, I pray for God's healing of your broken heart, that he binds up your wounds and bring light where there is darkness. I pray that during this difficult season of your life, you remember that God is still present, giving you strength and walking you through your pain. He does not abandon us during suffering. I decree and declare that every insecurity, fear, selfish ambition, financial struggle, and past hurt is cast out in the mighty name of Jesus. Lord, provide us knowledge and self-assurance to be selective in our decision-making.

I have been in the military for twenty-three years, and I have learned how to adapt to pain and grow from it. During Basic Training, we learned how to use pain to develop confidence in our ability to problem-solve. No one gets married anticipating the moment they will sign divorce papers. I challenge you not to use the pain from your divorce as a crutch but figure out how you can use it to gain self-awareness and grow. Know that YOU can get through it; YOU must be strong and believe it! Remember that our God is greater than any doubt that clutters your mind and even the situation that may be currently consuming your mind. As you dive into this book, I want you to think about the following questions. What are you seeing as you walk through this process? Are you just seeing the stuff, hurt, pain, and disappointment? Can you get past this and get to the point where you see Jesus working in your life? My Friends, God has taken all the Broken parts of you to put together a beautiful picture.

Chapter 2

How does it feel?

Losing a spouse through an unsuccessful marriage can trigger grief responses. Grief is an emotional response to a breakup, divorce, or loss of someone close that causes acute pain: Loss of marriage entails a loss of companionship and shared experiences. It can also involve a loss of support financially, intellectually, socially, and emotionally. Grief often involves excessive emotions such as sadness and sometimes feelings of shock and numbness, or even denial and anger. It is saying goodbye or closing a chapter of life with a former spouse, and that crap hurts.

Divorce is like grief; it goes through many different stages and emotions, and we all handle these stages and emotions in a different manner. My friends, it is imperative that we learn how to identify the different stages of divorce so that we can properly manage our emotions and cope with the process. Taking ownership of your feelings and responsibility for how you work through them improves your quality of life and those around you. Friends, be mindful that taking responsibility for your emotions when they are precipitated by another individual's conduct does not suggest that you condone or justify that behavior. It really means that you embody your emotions, whatever they may be, barring pointing the finger elsewhere.

When I went through my divorce, I felt resentment, denial, confusion, frustration, anger, guilt, and fear, I became vindictive, and I was embarrassed for having a failed marriage. Not one but two failed marriages. I did not care to care. I felt like God did not see me, but I still had faith. I just existed by smiling through the pain. I am telling you not to suppress your feelings, hoping they will eventually go away because they do not.

Friends, let us talk about the stages of divorce and some emotions that you may have experienced. I want you to keep in mind that they do not happen in any particular order, and you may or may not go through all of these stages. I call these stumbling blocks that we all need to watch out for.

Denial is our way of telling ourselves that something did not happen. While doing my research, I found out that many grief experts suggest that denial is sometimes our way of coping with traumatic and overpowering emotions that stem from the shock of a loss.

Denial sometimes causes us to put on a temporary defense mechanism mask in order to help us process things. Friends, if we take a moment to think about this stage, one party in the marriage is more than likely going to refuse to accept the fact that the marriage is ending because it is too painful. Which party are you? Have you taken the time to identify and deal with this stage in the process? Listen, we have identified that divorce can affect us spiritually, emotionally, and physically so this stage can also bring hope to some of us. It may have us thinking that our spouse may have a change of heart because they may be going through a phase.

During this phase, we must be careful and patient, especially if you are not the one that is filing for the divorce. You may experience avoidance, paperwork being postponed, and unexplainable fights. In my experience with this process, it happened after the initial shock that my marriage was ending. I filed for divorce, yet I still went through the denial stage. For one of my former spouses, the denial process was different from mine because he was not in agreement with the marriage ending. Before you ask," Did we try to work it out?" Yes, we did, and I just could not get over the trauma, so I decided to go my way. He was slow to respond because he was angry and trying to deal with his emotions as well. Once I acknowledged his circumstances, I gained a little patience because, truth be told, I felt really bad for him.

Anger is a common emotion many of us feel when experiencing a divorce. It speaks to the intensity of affection that once existed in your marriage, and when that ended, there seemed to be a lack of expression for the sudden change in the physical, mental, and emotional makeup of your life. Feeling angry during emotional pain protects us from feeling pity toward ourselves. If we think of anger as a survival stage, it will be easier to allow ourselves to feel it, identify it, and enable the feeling to take place. Friends, I encourage you to turn your anger into positive thinking because allowing it to place us in a negative space can be detrimental. Repressed anger is detrimental to our ability to grow and heal. When we do not deal with anger properly, it can cause long-term effects in our relationships because we take our anger out on the people we love, such as other family and friends. Now, do not get me wrong, some things warrant us the right to be angry, but we have to learn how to handle our anger. Friends, let us think about this, we are leaving a part of our lives behind. For some of you, it may be two or three years, and for others, it could be fifteen to thirty. Was I angry? You bet I was. I was angry because of the hurt from the betrayal, infidelity, and emotional abuse. Can I tell you that I was also angry at myself for allowing myself to be mistreated?

Divorce is like riding a roller coaster, mixed with so many emotions that will leave you confused, tired, and paralyzed with fear. Fear may be one of the top emotions experienced during a divorce because you are starting over. Your children, home, finances, family, mutual friends, and for some, pets are all affected. This usually creates anxiety even if you are the one that initiated the divorce. You may have questions like; What is going to happen now? How will I make it? Will it affect my children? Let us not forget about the thoughts that consume our minds about managing our finances, being alone, and being socially paralyzed.

The thought of my marriage ending made me relive memories and experiences that held me captive and overwhelmed me with thoughts of maybes, regrets, and disappointments. Friends, it was during my place of being stuck that I found comfort and relief once I realized that I was not the first woman about to experience a divorce. I used this experience to help me grow and develop as a woman and an individual. I challenge you to find a way to use your fears to help you gain knowledge and as an opportunity for you to live according to your terms.

Shame…Oh, the shame, friends, this is so real. There are many reasons why people feel guilt or shame. Some of us feel shame for "failing" at our marriages or putting on a front for people for too long for what I call saving face. In addition, some of us feel shame for being unfaithful or for having a spouse that was unfaithful to us. Research suggests that guilt stems from the feeling that you did not fulfill a promise to a loved one, did not hold up your end of the bargain, or ignored vital elements that could have modified the outcome. Guilt is usually the result of believing you should or could have done more or the result of having done something that caused damage to your relationship.

My reason for shame stems from the values that I grew up with. I was ashamed of having a failed marriage despite my biblical views. I felt guilty because I thought that if I had done things differently, it would have saved my marriage. I had shame from infidelity issues and people's views and talks about me for walking away. Your reasons may be similar to mine, and they may differ from mine. Whatever your reason is, some level of guilt is ok, but we cannot allow it to control us or become toxic.

The fear of being alone can be a contributing factor in causing recently divorced individuals to get into serious, often unhealthy, relationships. Which only makes sense because of the dramatic lifestyle change. Loneliness creeps in slowly, but I want you to remember that this is a temporary emotion that is part of the process of your healing.

Depression after a divorce is the process of feeling hopeless and overwhelmingly sad. This can bring on loneliness and cause many of us to feel as if we have no vision of our future. It is like being in a dark tunnel with no line of sight, thus creating vulnerability. During this stage, our Naked Truth is revealed, and the vision of the life you once had planned out no longer exists. Now, friends, this pain can feel unbearable but know that God will not give you anything he did not equip you to handle. Get your cry on and out, but do not allow yourself to become the victim. I want you to take some time to answer the following questions.

- Are you struggling to get out of bed?
- Are you acknowledging or suppressing your feelings?
- Are you isolating yourself?
- Are you having thoughts of harming yourself?
- Do you no longer have an interest in your hobbies?
- Have you seen an increase or decrease in your appetite or sleep schedule?

The acceptance stage means you acknowledge that the relationship is over and that there is a new chapter ahead. Friends, did you hear me? Acceptance means that it is

OVER, it brings closure, and YOU can "MOVE ON." Some of us may never get to this stage but let me tell you, it was during this stage that I realized that I could dry my tears, activate the strong woman inside of me and stop thinking about my ex. It may not mean that everything is magically fine overnight, but it does mean that you have accepted your reality.

Friends, I am about to give you all some coping skills that may help you to deal with the stages of divorce. They may help you move from a place of being stuck because these skills definitely helped me move forward. My suggestions are to first learn how to be patient with yourself because this is not an overnight process or fix. It may take some time for you to process and heal from each of these stages. Reach out for help. God knows that we all need it at times. Talk to a therapist and kill the myths that only crazy people need therapy. People who tend to suppress their emotions can also unintentionally prolong their duration of grief. Healing cannot start until one's emotions are acknowledged, understood, and dealt with.

Here are some things that helped me along the way, and I challenge you to try a few of these routines.

- Start planning. If you are still in the process of divorce, it may be difficult for you to think about anything else at this moment.

- Do not be afraid of socializing.

- Create your bucket list to do those things that you wanted to do and could not do when you were married.

- Go to the gym.

- Get yourself a journal and list all of the feelings you want to release concerning your divorce. I talked to a licensed therapist, and journaling was one of the best pieces of advice that she could offer me. Writing things out really helped me to put things into perspective and free myself.

- Do things that you enjoy.

- I have always been a woman with longer-than-average hair. After my divorce, I wanted a fresh start from my past of failed relationships. I cut my hair to ear length and shocked everyone.

Yes, friends, I know that divorce signifies the cease of a union. But I want you to know that you are in charge of the effects that it has on you. There may be instances when you feel trapped by the negative emotions of anger, guilt, fear, and depression; I need you to understand that divorce does not have to be a terrible experience. Divorce can be empowering and a positive catalyst for growth as it can provide both parties with new beginnings. Yes, there will be some bumps in the road ahead, and you may experience some turbulence as you are both navigating an emotional direction which can leave you feeling vulnerable, defensive, and afraid. When turbulence is anticipated or suddenly encountered, your Captain, Jesus, will turn on the FASTEN SEATBELT sign.

Let's Reflect:

Am I in denial?

Am I dealing with anxiety or depression?

What can I do to overcome it?

Is it hard for me to express my emotions? Am I able to handle them?

Do I need therapy?

Chapter 3

To Thine Own Self Be True

Self-Honesty is the practice of always speaking and acting in accordance with what you believe to be true, even if it's unpleasant or inconvenient. Fred Rogers said it best, "Honesty is often very hard, and the truth is often painful, but the freedom it can bring is worth the trying."

Hello friends, being honest with yourself is not easy, but it is necessary. Now, let me let you all in on something if you have not already picked up on it. I have been married and divorced not once but twice. Between the two previous marriages, I was married for a total of twelve years. Although I experienced some hardships, not all our time together was bad because we also had some great times. But friends, you know that thing called "Woman's Intuition," I suggest you pay a little more attention to it. I ignored it just like I ignored the red flags in the last chapter and the changes in routine. Why do you ask? Because I was hoping that I was wrong, and I did not want to be the cause of an argument or the blame for a damaged relationship. I experienced lying, infidelity, financial issues, blame, manipulation, a physical altercation, and mental and emotional abuse during this time. I was also criticized for not working out and turned into someone I did not even recognize. I started to overlook details, names, suspicions, lies, and mistreatment.

I struggled to figure out whom to blame for this nightmare that turned us into faceless animals. Friends, when this happens, we sometimes start to blame others because we choose not to admit that this is who we have become. I encourage you to take a moment to look back at your life prior to your marriage or relationship. Before your relationship, you considered yourself a solid person with your own values, and you were not looking for anyone to validate you. You were thoughtful, kind, caring, loving, and empathic. Then you got into a relationship, and the things that you thought you had gotten over surfaced at a degree that you did not see arising. You started telling yourself that your relationship will get better when your spouse gets his act together. Not realizing your spouse has simply exposed another layer of what was already unhealed in you.

We enter relationships wounded in many ways that we are unaware of until it is exposed. We become so good at compartmentalizing things to stay sane or make someone else look good. We begin to carry all this stuff on our backs that do not belong to us, and we need to learn how to let go of it. Erika Badu calls this the "bag lady." We chose not to accept that we all have blind spots, and as a result, we burn our relationships to the ground. There is only so much belittling, pain, arguing, going to bed angry, and frustration that we can take before we are so broken that we have no energy to do what is needed to repair things. Friends, let me help you; just STOP and gather yourself! Now Erika tells us that we must stop carrying around all of this baggage or we will hurt our backs.

Listen, I was hurting, and my mind frame was "hurt people hurt people." Yes, I was that chick! That should not be your motto. I wanted him to hurt because I was hurting. I wanted him to know what it felt like even though I knew that was not of God. Because I received infidelity, I wanted him to feel it, also. I was in the mind frame that I would cheat, but I would do it better. I became a hot mess, and only God's grace kept me from self-sabotage. Why do we try to fight our own battles when God has already fought and won these battles for us? Friends, I want to caution you from having this mindset. We are ladies of virtue and must learn how to fight with our spiritual weapons, not physical ones. Hurt people know how it feels to be in pain, so hurt people should do their best to help bring comfort to hurting people.

At times when we are in a place of hurt, we tend to build emotional walls that put a barrier between people with good intentions because we cannot see beyond past hurts. This makes us defensive and unable to foster authentic relationships. These emotions are completely normal but be careful not to allow yourself to be victimized and seek help. From one Queen to another, you can get through it; you just have to be strong and believe.

Once I realized that I was in this very mind frame, I developed self-awareness and began to take accountability and responsibility for myself and my actions. I no longer allowed myself to be a victim in an unhealthy relationship. I knew I had to start taking control of my thoughts, feelings, actions, and how I spoke. Friends, I mean that I had to really look at myself in the mirror because we are so quick to blame others without doing a self-reflection.

Self-honesty is not putting yourself down or feeling sorry for yourself. It is taking a magnified-glass approach to look at things as they are and then making a significant change for the better. Without self-awareness, we will keep repeating the same mistakes. You know the saying, "When you know better, you do better." Well, this applies because doing a self-reflection and truly being honest with yourself creates an opportunity for you to truly learn yourself and expose the areas that you need to improve. I was once told that there are two ways that people live in self-denial about who they are; one is assuming that they are better than they actually are, and two is that they constantly devalue themselves. Neither of which is a good look if you ask me.

Friends, I want to encourage you to pause for a moment and review the following self-reflection questions, take some time to think about your responses, and then answer them.

- How am I feeling right now?
- Am I being true to myself?

- Why did I respond that way?

- Is this the best way for me to deal with this situation?

- Am I happy?

- What am I grateful for?

- What do I not like about myself?

- Do I care too much about other people?

- Am I doing what's best for myself?

- Am I communicating in a manner that expresses my concerns?

If we are not honest with ourselves, it will prevent us from healing. If you lie to yourself, you will lie to others. I had become what I titled earlier, a faceless animal. I had lost all the unique characteristics that God had given me. I had become numb, and I lacked interest in my marriage. I had to be honest with myself about my faults in the relationship instead of placing all the blame on my spouse. I had to own my mistakes because, baby girl, we all have them, and if you think that this does not apply to you, you are lying to yourself. I stopped shrugging off my feelings because my feelings matter, just like the next person. I sought wise counsel and asked my loved ones to give me their honest opinions of my actions. Be careful with this one because you cannot ask those people you know will tell you what you want to hear. Be ready to receive some feedback that may not be so appealing, or it may not feel all warm and fuzzy.

Being honest with ourselves is not always an easy task, but it is required to keep us from repeating the same cycles. I am sure I am not the only person who has been married and divorced more than once. Part of my self-reflection required me to look at the mistakes I made in my first and second marriages and other relationships to see my faults and how I could improve my actions to get a different result. I know that we typically call these failed marriages, but I realized that they taught me some things about myself and gave me two amazing little humans whom I love so dearly.

Here are a few things I learned; your spouse is not responsible for making you happy, and you are not responsible for making them happy. Happiness is found within. You should try to avoid conflict by addressing things head-on instead of trying to find a diversion or bottling things up in preparation for the next explosion.

You cannot change your spouse; leave that to God. Always speak the truth because lies only make things more complicated. Heal and get rid of your baggage before saying, "I do." Learn who you are and whose you are. Know your value and add tax! I also learned the importance of communication, dating, and intimacy. Honesty is one of our greatest values because it is a necessary attribute for us to grow and build trust.

Divorce can often cause us to feel powerless and helpless, but the information is power. You may have suffered for a little while, but God's word says in 1 Peter 5:10 that he will restore, support, and strengthen you and place you on a firm foundation. "You can never be true to others if you keep on lying to yourself." — Gift Gugu Mona

Let's Reflect:

Am I an honest person?

Do I trust my judgment?

Am I fighting a battle that has already been won?

Have I been honest with myself?

Do I tend to overreact to things?

Chapter 4

Ready, Re-set, Grow

When we go through a divorce or traumatic experiences, it feels like we lose sight of our peace. Healing is a very personal journey, and it requires courage. For some of us, we are healing from neglect or emotional, verbal, and physical abuse. But God's word tells us in Philippians 6-7 "not to worry but instead to pray about everything." Then we will experience God's peace, which exceeds anything we can understand and guard our hearts and minds. God is the God of peace, and he wants you and I to receive his peace, and in order to experience this peace, we must properly heal. God is the true answer to our complete healing, peace, and wholeness.

Internal Healing begins when you change your thoughts about whom you think you are. Your thoughts spark positivity and create hope, thus influencing your journey to healing. We are all faced with challenges and stressors at some point in our lives, but we get to decide how we respond.

Healing is defined as the process of making or becoming sound or healthy again. Biblically it means; Healing occurs through the integrating forces that restore, transform, sustain, and nurture the whole person (body, mind, spirit) at each phase and in every dimension of life, and within relationships of the person to the creation, to other people, and God "Taylor H, 2007, Sent to Heal. A handbook on Christian healing." Are you in a place where you are wondering if healing from your emotional wounds is possible? Perhaps you have been in this place for a while and feel stuck, broken, defeated, or overwhelmed. Well, Friend, I want to encourage you today that emotional healing is possible.

Do you feel like you will never recover from the hurt, loss, or betrayal? Well, it's time to change your story. Instead of focusing on the hurt, what if we realize that the things that hurt us also give us power and empower us to be stronger? The moment you do this, you can start to transform what was once broken into something beautiful. How do you begin the transformation process? You take the time to begin healing. If you try to rush the healing process, you are only setting yourself up for failure. You must be willing to do the work, embrace setbacks, and sometimes circle back to some lessons until you've fully learned from them.

My healing journey went a little something like this. Whoever said that divorce is not a big deal is straight-up lying. It became worse before it became better. The manipulation, lies, jabs, and yelling all became too much. I distanced myself from my former spouse. I cried, and I cried until I could not cry anymore. I reminded myself over and over about the betrayal. I prayed, but I must admit that my prayer life was not what it is today. I begin to seek counsel and journal to write out my feelings instead of suppressing them.

Yes, the days and nights were long, but each day became easier and easier. My hurt and pain started to dissolve. I realized the same grace God gives me every day that I had to extend to my former spouses. How do we choose not to forgive when Christ has forgiven us? Unforgiveness will keep you from healing. For us to experience God's forgiveness, we need to extend the same forgiveness to others, even when we can't forget what they've done. Let God give you the strength and empathy required for you to forgive. I had to forgive the things that had been said to me and the actions taken toward me. Once I forgave, it became easier to have those interactions with my former spouse without the arguments and low blows.

Michelle Cameron wrote 'When you can look at your pain and share it with others without falling apart; when you can laugh with the person who made you cry almost daily; and when you can love your child without anger at his other parent, forgiveness, and healing has definitely taken place.' Whew, chile, if this statement right here is not the truth, I do not know what is.

Invisible wounds are real; you cannot heal if you keep pretending you aren't hurt. When you do not take the time to heal, over time, it spills out on other people that had nothing to do with you being hurt. You can be beautiful on the outside and ugly on the inside. You can be the prettiest person to others yet feel like the ugliest. Trust me; I have been there. Stop letting people have so much control that they plant insecurities in your life. Now friends, my healing journey took some time, and yours will also. Once I realized that I was walking around with a cast on beyond the point of being healed, I accepted that my marriage had ended and refocused my energy.

Now, for those who have had a broken bone or two, you know that you do not want to keep that cast on longer than you need to. It starts to stink really bad and itch something awful. As a kid, I remember my dad had a cast on his leg. That leg was itching him so badly that he would grab a metal coat hanger and undo it until it was straight to scratch it. We must not have had insurance or the money for him to get it taken off because he just could not wait. So, he ended up cutting that bad boy off himself (lol). Let us learn a lesson from my dad, do not be afraid to remove the cast once you have reached your healing point. I encourage you to learn how to love yourself again. True love is within and not found in another person. Let your light SHINE from within so that it cannot be DIMMED!

Lord, I ask that you touch every woman reading this book. Give them a spirit of peace and love. Let the woman reading this book know that she is enough and that you are in control of every situation. Heal her from her past and open her up to emotional vulnerability so that she can experience complete healing.

You can't stay stuck. Having your own pity party. You must move past the shame, guilt, and hurt. When your future is greater than your past, you have no choice but to keep it moving forward! My friend, God is a right now God. Your situation is unique for God to do something in your life. He sometimes allows things to die to get our attention and put the focus back on him. You know that our God is a jealous God. God's word tells us in Isaiah 53:5, "that he was pierced for our rebellion, crushed for our sins. He was beaten so we could be whole. He was whipped so we could be healed." Sis, years of pain are not your portion. So, what are you waiting on to receive your healing?

Heal so that your wounds can become scars. Do you know the difference between wounds and scars? Wounds cause affliction, and scars are a reminder that you were once wounded and healed from it. Stop picking the scabs off, causing those wounds to resurface. Learn how to forgive. Forgiveness does not mean that it did not happen or that it did not hurt, but it brings you closure. Your greatest strengths are shown through your scars. Remember, they nailed Jesus to the cross and that he was wounded for our transgressions. His scars are a reminder that what hurts us no longer holds us. To receive freedom, you must LET It Go! Tell yourself that you will no longer stay in that place of hurt.

How do you heal emotionally? Well, I am glad you asked.

- Take baby steps.
- Recognize that it's ok to have different feelings; acknowledge these feelings.
- Remember that you do not have to heal 100% to improve the quality of your life.
- Be patient and persistent.
- Set realistic expectations.
- Don't go through this alone.
- View setbacks as part of the process and learning opportunities.
- Prioritize self-care and self-compassion.
- Be willing to process your feelings about the past.
- Ask for help.

Can I share something with you? You are uniquely loved! God loves each and every one of us so much that he sacrificed his only son for our sins. How many of us would have been willing to do the same? I have two sons, and I could not imagine having to let my sons die for other people's sins, especially those that do not like, love, or even know them. Think about that for a moment. How many of us would sacrifice anything to extend grace to each other? Not many of us, right, so this shows us just how much God loves us. In return, he expects us to show ourselves and others that same love and grace. God knows and loves each of us individually. If that does not show you enough Grace. God loved us enough to pay our debts. Think about all the debt you are currently in right now and imagine if someone walked up to you and handed you a stack of cash that covered your debt. Some of you would be screaming and shouting. Jesus did not hand you a stack of cash, but he paid your debts with his life! Friends, you are healed! God's word says that by his stripes, we are healed. He took the beatings and bruises for us so that we would not have to suffer.

Move past the hurt so that you can experience true healing. Ask yourself, how can I use this to make me better. Remember, you do not have to suffer in silence. I challenge you to start your day with elevated emotions such as gratitude, joy, love, and peace. Thank God for all he has and is doing in your life. Start to command your mornings, as this will immediately elevate your energy and be an astonishing start to your day. When you wake up in the morning, think of a few things you are grateful for, say a quick prayer, or write a journal entry. Gratitude is a great way to put things into perspective and remind you of what is important in life.

Let's Reflect:

Do I believe that healing from emotional
wounds is possible?

How can I use my hurt and pain to gain
strength?

Do I blame myself? How can I let go of guilt?

Chapter 5

Reboot & Let Me Re-introduce Myself

1 Peter 5:10 And the God of all grace, who called you unto his eternal glory in Christ, after that, ye have suffered a little while, shall himself perfect, establish and strengthen you. "Forget the former things, do not dwell on the past. See, I am doing a new thing!"

Sometimes we all just need to Reboot. The Oxford Dictionary tells us that rebooting means to restart or revive; it gives fresh impetus. I do not know about you all, but I love the word REVIVE because it makes me think of new life. Regrets and shame are two powerful words that tend to cripple many of us daily. What is life without them? Holding on to these emotions can hinder us from enjoying life's blessings. Guess what? The great news is that you can escape the "Regretful Sequence" of regrets, shame, and disappointments and start over. Say Good-Bye to fear, shame, and regrets and hello to God's promises. We are given the chance to be redeemed through God's grace. This is an opportunity for you to discover yourself.

Rebooting is the process by which a running computer system is restarted. Just like that computer, you have gone through the shutdown phase of your divorce, and now it is time for a restart. The purpose of restarting is to improve your current situation. Yes, we all can admit that divorce is a difficult situation to go through and that it can take a mental toll on the strongest person. Causing the need for a Reboot because, like Fantasia says, "It's necessary."

After going through those negative emotions, it is necessary to install system updates, recover from hurts, and re-initialize your drive or passion. A simple restart refreshes your memory registers, making them ready to start over again. Rebooting is simply the process of closing one chapter of your life and starting over with a new chapter. When you choose not to reboot, your mind becomes slower over time because it is bogged down with memories of regrets, failure, shame, and disappointments. Rebooting helps flush all those temporary files piled up in your memory bank so you can operate in your newness.

Knowing what to expect with divorce and proper preparation can make your transition to restarting smoother. In addition, excepting the adjustment periods will help you move forward. Remember, your life is still yours! SIS, if you are in this moment, HOLD ON because better days are coming. You can change the trajectory of your story. Here are some helpful tips to help you manage and prepare.

- Discuss the Divorce. Try to remain calm and have these conversations in a neutral place.

- Get Support. Trusted individuals and not people just trying to be in your business.

- Hire an Attorney but do your research because you don't want just any attorney; you need to understand your rights.

- Sort out the Separation Details.

- Make Plans for the Children. Like visitation and child support (should there be any).

- Itemize Your Belongings. Personal items and jointly owned items.

- Compile Your Legal Documents. Remember to change those insurance policies and beneficiaries.

- Organize Your Financial Paperwork. Try to keep all your documents together for easier access.

The thought of starting over for me alone was heart-aching. Questions like, where do I begin? How will I make it financially without a second income? How will my children be affected? How will I navigate my life after my divorce? So on and so forth. Friends, I am going to let you all in on a little something because my life was not always what it is now. Once my divorce was final, I got with my girls, and we went out to celebrate, and boy, did we celebrate. Those became my hot girl days. Once the celebration was over, I was happy and sad. You know the saying. "To get over one, you get under another." Well, that is what I did. Chile, I was young and dumb. As we used to say when we were kids, Please Pretty Please with a cherry on top, learn from my mistakes, and do not do that. But then I had to look at it from a different perspective.

I became educated, sought advice, and began living my best life. I am guessing by now you all have picked up on the fact that I love music. Well, these words below from a song titled "Destiny" by Kevin Lamar helped me get through this rough patch. "This is not a time to get distracted. This is not a time to go off course. This is not a time to lose your focus. You cannot afford to lose your way. You've come too far from where you started from. Your destiny is too important to give up for anything." Your destiny is extremely important, and for you to reach it, sometimes it takes a reboot or adjustment when you are out of alignment. I have included some tips to help you as you begin your Reboot:

- Start with self-reflection.
- Examine your value system.

- Revisit (and rewrite) your goals. Make them attainable.

- Work up the courage to change.

- Make your next move. Boss Up!

- Get a coach.

- Get you a sister circle. God knows that I am thankful for mine.

An unsuccessful marriage may cause you to develop hostility with yourself or the other person. Prayerfully it is not to the point where you are harming yourself. If so, please seek help immediately. Think about this, divorce brings on anger, and that anger is sometimes warranted. However, a lot of our anger and feelings are temporary. We must be careful not to let our anger and feelings negatively influence the result of the divorce or mutilate family relationships. I am sure you have heard the saying, "Don't make a permanent decision based on temporary feelings." You must stop being hostile and change the narrative. Remember, you drive the change that is necessary to Reboot! Take a look at these critical tips that I think are needed when going through a hostile divorce.

- Have Patience.

- Demonstrate Honesty.

- Think before you speak.

- Nurture yourself – remember that you matter.

- Focus on your kids.

- Remain calm.

- Get legal counsel.

While I was rebooting, I also developed a better relationship with God and learned about the power of forgiveness that we talked about in a previous chapter. Forgiveness is not always about only forgiving the other person. Many times, we need to learn how to forgive ourselves as well. With forgiveness, you can regain your sense of self. Forgiving someone that has harmed you frees you of pain, anger, hurt, bitterness, and shame; those very things that keep you from starting over and moving forward with your life. It also gives you the ability to be understanding, show empathy, and give grace and compassion to those who have harmed you. I noticed that once I was able to truly forgive, I was no longer the victim. We all have pulled the victim card at some point in our lives, whether we were the true victim or not. Staying stuck in the victim role is not healthy. I say this because it implants fear, prevents you from moving forward, and renders you powerless. Sis, we know that we women are some powerful creatures! If you victimize yourself, you are refuting your power to change things and putting your future into someone else's hands, and that could be like playing

Russian roulette. That would be a Hard Pass for me! Stop placing the blame on your spouse or ex-spouse. While the accusations may be true, we still had a part in the relationship even if we were in denial and chose to ignore the warning signs or take responsible action.

I encourage you to be responsible for your own life and take back your control. Ask yourself these two questions, what am I gaining from being the victim? Am I afraid to face the truth? I will admit I thought that although things were true if I allowed myself to remain the victim, then people would side with me. I was also afraid at times to face the truth about how irresponsible I was in my marriage.

"People that hold onto hate for so long do so because they want to avoid dealing with their pain. They falsely believe if they forgive, they are letting their enemy believe they are a doormat. What they don't understand is hatred can't be isolated or turned off. It manifests in their health, choices, and belief systems. Their values and religious beliefs make adjustments to justify their negative emotions. Not unlike malware infesting a hard drive, their spirit slowly becomes corrupted, and they make choices that don't make logical sense to others. Hatred left unaddressed will crash a person's spirit. The only thing he or she can do is to reboot by fixing him or herself, not others. This might require installing a firewall of boundaries or parental controls on their emotions. Regardless of the approach, we are all connected on this "network of life," and each of us is responsible for cleaning up our spiritual registry." — Shannon L. Alder

Let me tell you a quick story. A cousin of mine was married to a narcissist who constantly demanded that things go his way. He dismissed her thoughts and feelings and displayed no empathy for her. He always seemed to be irritated and angry. Which often left her frustrated because he never understood her intentions and he was never pleased. She was in a place where it felt as if her foot was stuck in the sand, and she could not move. This type of behavior not only affects your self-confidence but also affects your connection with other people, your identity, and your individual needs, which results in a lack of motivation to move forward. If you are not careful or identify it early enough it could potentially create mental health concerns, such as anxiety and depression. I can proudly say that my cousin was able to come face to face with the truth, forgive her ex, and make some changes that ignited her reboot, and today she is unbothered and living her best life.

Knowing that you need a restart and remaining hostile and stuck in unforgiveness is like falling into quicksand. GET UP out of that quicksand. How do you survive quicksand? "The more you lean back, the more it'll help bring your legs to the surface. Then you can move yourself to the side of the pit. And get yourself to safety." In the case of divorce, leaning back is utilizing the tips and resources that have been given to you, preparing your mind to start your Reboot, and overcoming hostility through forgiveness. You are now on solid ground; welcome to safety. Get Up! Nobody is going to go hard after what you want but you. God promised it to us already, and now all you have to do is go get it. I need you to believe that RESTORATION is your portion and be willing to be a beginner every morning.

Let's Reflect:

Am I holding onto things that I need to let go of?

Am I ready to move forward?

Am I resisting forgiveness? Why?

Am I letting things that I can't control cause me
to stress?

Will I allow unforgiveness to keep me bound?

Chapter 6

No Co-pilot

I decided that instead of being embarrassed about my unsuccessful marriage and ashamed of being a single mother, I was going to OWN it.

When I started writing my book, I surveyed divorced mothers, and the number one concern was how the divorce would affect my children. As I mentioned earlier in the book, when I was growing up, all I thought about was getting married and having children. I mean I loved kids so much; I would play with everyone, and I even started thinking that I would be a pediatrician until that one college professor messed that thought up. For me, it did not happen in that order because I had my son out of wedlock and was married to my first husband several months later. But the thought of getting divorced and raising my kids alone never crossed my mind.

My childhood consisted of my two siblings and me, and my parents are still married to this day, and that is what I wanted for my kids. I can admit that the decision to divorce is especially complicated when children are involved because you have to consider your feelings and desires and theirs. I know that many people choose to stay married for the sake of their children, and that is their business. Yes, I thought about it and tried. I do not advocate for divorce, and I believe you should try to avoid it at all costs. But I also thought about how many children are affected by witnessing abusive, conflicted, and unhappy marriages full of anger and frustration.

Some experts say that it is better to stay married because children tend to flourish in predictable, secure households with two parents. I believe that children can flourish in any healthy household where there are one or two parents present. They also say that divorce is disturbing, stressful, and destabilizing. While I agree, I also believe that unhealthy marriages can be equally stressful and disturbing to children.

Studies have shown that children that grow up in unhealthy and conflicting homes may have a hard time developing positive self-esteem, forming and sustaining relationships, and managing their emotions. One piece of advice that I would give if your children were old enough to understand is please talk to them and advise them of the decision for you and your spouse to separate. What was most important for me was making sure that my children were cared for and that they received less stress as possible because divorce can be emotional for them as well. One of the biggest challenges we face as parents that choose to divorce is making sure that we both learn how to work together for the sake of the children, as this tends to make things a bit less painful.

In a perfect world, both parents would be able to come together and raise the kids without any issues, but the world is not perfect. I must admit that in the beginning working together may not be as cohesive as you would like. Because it is sometimes hard to push past disagreements, hurt, and anger. Now, come on, sis, if you are anything like me, at times, we can just be extra petty. But for us to effectively co-parent, we must find a way to develop a new respectful relationship that is built on communication. Now, both of my divorces had their own share of challenges when it came down to the kids and us working together. Our issue was never a custody battle, and I never tried to keep either ex from spending time with my kids, so that may be your story for another book, but it is not mine. But we had our own hurts and disappointments, and it was hard to communicate without feelings, heightened emotions, or exposing pain. When this happens, one or the other parent may not be as involved with the children because they cannot stomach the other parent. Let me tell you that it is very frustrating, to say the least. But let me help you out; you are not responsible for changing anyone or their behavior. So do you and take care of your kids! Let us discuss a few issues that I did have.

I remember trying so hard to step in for the other parent when he chose to be absent. I caused undue stress on myself by purchasing items and Christmas gifts and putting his name on them so my kids would not feel neglected because he would tell them that their gifts were in the mail, but we know they never came. Sis, you do not have to do this. Being an authentic parent does not require you to take on the role of someone else. Another issue was my ex taking the divorce out on my children. What I mean by that is that he stopped showing up and being present for them.

One last issue I had was when one of my ex's decided to remarry and wanted my children to call his wife "mom." That ate me up to the bottom of my core. Did I curse and scream and call him and go off? Yes, I did. Later, the mature me had to have self-talk. I said self, if she is a good and respectful woman, why are you tripping because you want someone in their life that will treat them as their own? I had a conversation with my children to ensure that they were ok and that they were not being forced to call their "Bonus Mom," mom, and once I received confirmation from them, I was relieved.

Listen, friends, this may still be a touchy subject for you, but I want you to remember that your kids can never replace you as their mother. It is not a competition, and your children should not have to choose which set of parents to love. Your concern, as was mine is to make sure that your kids are protected, cared for, and loved. It is so many crazy people out here in this world, and I realized that my children are blessed to have other people in their lives to help raise, guide, and love them just as I do.

Some things for you to take into consideration:

- Do not let other people's opinions sway you.

- Forgive yourself for the mistakes you're bound to make.

- Improve your working relationship with your ex, and never talk bad about them in front of your kids.

- Keep a positive attitude.

- Attend to your child's needs.

- Take some time for yourself. You deserve it.

"It takes a village to raise a child." Well, I created my village and made sure that I was intentional with my children to ensure they felt loved.

Divorce causes so much change and chaos that it is hard to adjust - for us and our children. We become exhausted trying to maintain and keep up. One of the most difficult parts about being a divorced single mother is that, before divorce, there were two parents sharing the responsibilities of children. As a single mother, there is exponentially more work every single day, especially if we are the primary custody single parent, and it seems like the days are not long enough. Even in this, you must learn how to make time for yourself because you will experience BURN OUT. Creating schedules is a tremendous help to maximizing your time and getting your kids involved.

Establishing routines and rules fosters consistency, structure, and stability during these times of uncertainty as well as reducing stress.

- Create household routines. I remember people saying." Your kids know how to wash and fold clothes?" I'm like, yes, yours don't?

- Get them involved in school or sports activities.

More importantly, let your child express themselves. Build a strong support system around your children and maintain a sense of safety and unconditional love.

Minimize the conflict and negative effects of divorce on your children's lives by making their lives as normal as possible. If you are blessed to co-parent, some things can help you minimize the drama.

- Schedule Dropoff and Pickup Times

- Choose a neutral location.

- Discuss discipline so the children are playing you both or against one another.

- Holiday and weekend schedules. Be prepared for the other parent not to uphold their end.

- Bedtimes

Sometimes it takes us being like Yosemite trees. They can be as big as about 25 feet and around 300 feet tall, with a root base of 10 feet. How do they withstand wind, storms, and fire? Their roots are intertwined, and they feed nutrients to each other, producing strength that helps each of them to stand strong. You do not have to do this alone. God's word says, "Do not fear for I am with you; do not be dismayed, for I am your God. I will strengthen you and uphold you with my righteous hand" Isaiah 41:10. Lean in on your support system and be the best mother you can be.

Let's Reflect:

Am I meeting my expectations as a mother?

Have I set boundaries?

Do I accept help from my support system?

Do I avoid taking care of myself because I
feel unworthy?

Do I allow my kids to run the show because I
blame myself?

Chapter 7

Funny Money Or Strange Change

"Breathe, Beautiful. This is just a chapter of your life; it is not your whole story."

One of the biggest issues we struggle with after a divorce is how to deal with our finances; divorce can be expensive. Managing your money after a divorce can seem overwhelming once you realize all your financial responsibilities as the sole breadwinner. In most cases, but not all, divorced mothers suffer more than men after a divorce.

This is why you must be smart and plan because you are at risk of losing your possessions, including those you may have had prior to the marriage, like your money, financial assets, home, vehicle, and incurring debt. Financial literacy and financial planning can help shield your assets and prepare you for moving forward as a single individual.

I must admit that while I was going through my process, I did not have all this knowledge until after the fact. This is my reason for sharing it with you as a means to help someone else. During the time I was going through my divorces (yes, it's plural), I was not working with much money, and I had several bills.

In one divorce, I moved back up to Atlanta, rented a townhome, took over a car payment, and paid back payday loans and rental furniture fees, all of which had been acquired within the marriage. I also had expenses for the kid's extracurricular activities and our everyday living costs, all while trying to rebuild my credit that had been severely damaged in my marriage.

In the other divorce, I left my home with nothing but my children's beds and our clothes. I rented an apartment and refurnished it, paid two car notes, the kid's extracurricular activities and credit card bills, etc. So, as you can see, I had to become organized and strategic with my spending habits. I realized there was no reason to cry over spilled milk because it did not change anything. Let me tell you something, crying alone does not change your situation; you must be willing to do the work and use the resources God gave you. You need some people in your life who will push you and not just cry with you. They need to be willing to help you get out of your mess or that stuck place in your life.

One of the first things I did was create a budget and learn how to live within my means. While creating my budget, I had to look at the amount of money I was bringing in versus what I had going out through payments for necessities and NICE-sities (you know, those extra things that are nice to have but aren't necessary). I had a savings account, but it was empty, so there were no emergency funds. I had to quickly cut those things that were not essential. That meant not going out, eating out, getting my hair and nails done until I could bounce back, and I am grateful to say that my bounce-back game was strong.

I am blessed to say that I bounced back by becoming debt free except for my car note and mortgage, paid that second car off, repaired my credit, established a savings account, and purchased a home. As a testimonial to show you that divorce does not have to break you and that you can survive life after a divorce, since that time, I have purchased a total of four homes and some land. You can't tell me that my God is not Great! Keep in mind that this process does not improve overnight. It takes a lot of hard work and effort on your part, and it might become emotional, especially when you look at your account statements versus your bills.

Yes, the divorce may change your standard of living temporarily but DO not give up, take it one day at a time, remain positive, utilize your resources, and keep moving forward. Change your mindset, "watch your thoughts because your thoughts become words, words become actions, actions become habits, habits become character, and character becomes your destiny' ~ Frank Outlaw. You can't be wealthy with a poverty mindset!

You can begin to shift your mindset and go from lack to abundance with the following. "How to Shift Your Money Mindset in 5 Easy Steps." My friend, abundance is your portion!

- Reflect on your financial perspective. How has your past influenced your view on money?

- Adopt a positive money mindset. How do you speak to yourself?

- Shift your mindset to save money. What are your financial goals and values?

- Monitor your spending. What are you spending your money on?

- Commit to changing your money habits. Are you willing to make some changes?

- Read books that will influence your mind in a positive way. Are you feeding your brain good food?

- Believe that success is possible for you. Do you believe your worth?

Financial planning can help protect your assets and prepare you for moving forward as the single bread-WINNER. Many women ask what ways I could be affected by my divorce financially. Well, it could affect each person in a different manner. In many situations, women lose their health insurance, financial stability, retirement plans, and their homes. It could also affect your credit score and credit card debt, but this does not have to be your story. Now perhaps you could be like me and decide that in order to have peace, you just leave everything and start from scratch. It was more important for me to protect my PEACE, and I chose not to exchange anything for it.

This process taught me how to become a go-getter to ensure my kids never went without. I won't say that they always had the best or were always able to eat what they wanted. I learned how to tap into resources and freed myself from financial bondage. Sis, look at it like this, you can use this challenge as an opportunity to design a new life by making positive lifestyle changes, developing your own financial goals, and ensuring that you work hard so that you are financially stable to enjoy the things you have always wanted to do.

I have heard and witnessed so many astonishing testimonies and creative things that many of us have done to tread water financially as single moms and heads of household. Some of those include opening restaurants or starting catering businesses out of their homes. Utilizing an empty room as an Airbnb or setting up a retail shop out of it. I found my love for baking during this time, and I begin to use my creativity to generate extra income for my household.

By my second divorce, I had been serving in the military for thirteen years. I realized that I was an experienced event and party planner, so I used this experience for my financial benefit. I also went back to school and received my Associate of Arts in Hospitality Management, also my Bachelor of Arts in Business, and later received my real estate license. If you are at a point in your life where you feel like you have no financial support and no immediate career to depend on, or you just need some extra income to make ends meet.

I encourage you to begin your financial freedom by reflecting on your God-given talents and experience you do have. I'm sure that as a mother, you have; chaired fundraisers, organized class parties, booked and set all activities for family vacations, managed home calendars, coordinated sports activities, cheerleading, tutoring, birthday parties, social events, and babysitters. Do not let this experience be wasted.

You have the opportunity to create financial health and protect yourself from what could be a financial nightmare.

- Knowing exactly what money we have coming in and going out.

- Having a savings account for emergencies
- Clear, consistent budgeting
- Balancing a checkbook or your account.
- Savings for special occasions
- Ensure that you have an account solely in your name. I have heard the nightmare of ex's transferring all the funds from the joint account into a personal account.

Educate yourself, and there is no education like adversity! US bank has a great article titled "5 financial considerations in a divorce" that can be found on the following article "Financial Considerations in a Divorce: U.S. Bank. "I believe it is a great read and worth your time.

- Take inventory of your assets and debts, both individually and jointly. Be sure to include things like loans, credit card accounts, business, and tax return information.
- Hire an experienced divorce attorney - especially if the divorce is contested.
- If you have retirement accounts, be prepared to split them. Just because your name is

on a 401(k), IRA, or TSP doesn't mean it's not up for grabs. These funds may be considered "marital property" and subject to negotiation.

- Sort out your mortgage, rent, or lease payments. Mortgage companies and landlords expect payments to be made regardless of your personal situation. My cousin is currently dealing with this, and although she is remaining in the home, she must send proof of payment to her ex every month.

- Sort out equity and be prepared to split it. Going through a divorce is life-changing and can be overwhelming. It can also be extremely challenging, both emotionally and financially. It is important for you to understand what your new financial situation may look like as a single individual. Do not continue to drown. Use this opportunity to become financially literate and develop a Mindset of abundance for lasting wealth. You have the power to change your mindset! To help you improve your mindset regarding your finances, I want you to start by doing this quick exercise found on https://wealthovernow.com/how-to-clean-up-your-money-mindset/.

- BREATHE!

- Write down all your thoughts about money.

- Identify the trends in your thoughts.

- Stop comparing yourself to others.

- Practice gratitude.

- Create a budget.

- Write down your financial goals.

Chapter 8

Unclaimed Freight

Many of us struggle to love ourselves, but in Jeremiah 31:3. God tells us that he loves us with everlasting love.

Self-worth is the internal sense of being good enough and worthy of love and belonging from others. Not to be confused with self-esteem. Self-esteem is how you value yourself; it is your thoughts, judgments, and feelings about yourself, all of which self-worth is at the core of. In my opinion, both equate to self-love, how we feel about ourselves, think about ourselves, and act toward ourselves. Meaning being on your own team and giving yourself the same respect, dignity, and understanding you want for your loved ones.

Like you, I have been there, and I know firsthand what it feels like to be embarrassed, to feel ashamed, to be criticized, heartbroken, cheated on, confused, angry, devastated, disappointed, depressed, devalued, selfless, tired, unappreciated, unworthy, unloved, and unwanted. I have been in your shoes, where I entered relationships I knew I had no business being in, but because I did not value myself, I allowed myself to do so. I felt like because

I was a divorced mother that no one would want me, so I just entertained anyone who came my way that was half decent.

I struggled with the very things that I loved about myself. I no longer loved myself and thought that there was something wrong with me. I was insecure with my body, and I compartmentalized myself. To be honest with you all, I still struggle with this sometimes, and social media will do this to us because of all the filters and such it makes us seem like we have to be perfect. I had to remind myself that God's word says I was made perfect in his image. I did not like my freckles, but today I see them as sprinkles of sunshine. I did not like how big my arms were or how they waved when I waved. I did not like the fact that I was and still am a part of the itty-bitty titty committee. I did not like my stomach and the scars left behind after having three surgeries. All of which caused me to lack self-confidence. My SCARS are a testament to my two beautiful blessings and a reminder that God healed me.

We, as humans, are constantly evaluating our worth based on what society says our worth should be or look like. Society says that our self-worth should be based on our appearance, material possessions, financial assets, social circle or status, careers, and achievements. Now, while all of these things may contribute to who we are, they do not define us. Take, for instance, our social status; it is enlightening to have people like you or follow you on social media; however, their opinions should not impact your innate value. Your worth is the same whether people like you or not.

This level of understanding begins with knowing who you are and creating ways to boost your self-acceptance. Remind yourself that your bank account, job title, attractiveness, and social media following have nothing to do with how valuable or worthy you are. Silence that inner critic that constantly reminds you of your flaws. Sis, you are FLAWSOME; you are Flawed but you are still Awesome. Some nurturing steps towards regaining your self-worth and ensuring that you are valued are as follows.

- Meditate. Pray.
- Develop better eating habits.
- Develop an exercise routine.
- Start Journaling.

- Speak positive affirmations to yourself. Affirmations help you maintain positivity.

- Learn to enjoy yourself. Take yourself out.

- Ask for help.

- Learn to say no.

It is understandable that we tend to let someone else's love for us encourage us to feel better about ourselves. However, you should work on feeling good about yourself. One person's view of you does not determine who you are, nor does it determine your value. We can learn how to evaluate our actions to grow versus our worthiness. We can do this by doing self-reflection to see how we perceive our worth. Ask yourself the following questions.

- Are there circumstances when I tend to compare myself to others?

- Are there circumstances in which I pretend to be someone else to gain acceptance?

- In what ways am I most critical of myself?
- What makes me feel like my sense of self-worth increases?
- In what circumstances do I feel most insecure?

Stop worrying about what other people think, get like Chloe, and tell 'em," "Don't worry about me, Ima. be all right. I got GOD...all over my life." Then you tell yourself the following:

- I am already LOVED.
- I am already CHOSEN.
- I know who I AM.
- I know what God has SPOKEN.
- I am ENOUGH.

"Why should we worry about what others think of us? Do we have more confidence in their opinions than we do our own?" ~Brigham Young

This is something that a friend of mine had to come to terms with because she was looking for her husband to validate her. She was so in love with being a wife and mother that when the marriage was taken away, her self-worth vanished, and she forgot who she was. Her thought pattern changed on whom she thought she wanted to be, and she stopped caring to care. She went from being naturally friendly to overly flirtatious until she was able to understand her worth. At times we tend to seek validation from others because we undervalue ourselves.

Get over yourself and get over the rejections. Remember that rejections build character. Okay, I will admit that rejection hurts. I am sure that you have been rejected once or twice from jobs, friends, dates, credit applications, car or home loans, and sports activities, but when it comes from your spouse, it hits you like a ton of bricks. That rejection alone can make anyone feel undervalued and leave you with self-esteem issues and emotional wounds. It also causes many of us to become bound by fear to protect ourselves from being rejected. If you enable rejection to damper your self-worth and hold you back from moving forward in life, it can have negative consequences. On a positive note, rejection can be used to empower you to grow and develop resiliency. It is so important for us to practice self-care and ensure that our surroundings foster positivity so that we do not slip into those negative feelings of depression. I encourage you to eliminate self-criticism, introduce self-compassion, and realize your WORTH.

To help you verify your self-worth, I encourage you to write out your feelings. Now, I have mentioned journaling a few times, and many of you may need to learn how to begin because I did not know how. I am going to tell you what my therapist told me. Start with writing down your daily thoughts and interactions. Write an entry that lists your strengths and values and begin every morning off by reading them out loud to yourself. The late Kobe Bryant said something that stuck with me. "At the end of each day, look yourself in the mirror and ask, did I get better today?" Of course, he was talking about basketball, but you can relate this to every area of your life towards improvement. Rejection is a part of life but do know you can overcome it. Here is a list of things you can do to overcome rejection "How to Deal with Rejection: 7 Tips."

- Recognize that rejection is a part of life. Some things aren't meant to be.

- Accept what happened. The worst way to cope with rejection is to deny it.

- Process your emotions.

- Treat yourself with compassion.

- Stay healthy.

- Don't allow rejection to define you.

- Grow from the experience.

Sis, your future is greater than your past; you have no choice but to keep it moving forward! You are worth it; God sacrificed his son Jesus's life, so that alone should show you that you are WORTHY of his promises! The moment that you understand accept and love yourself, you will reach a point where you no longer depend on people, accomplishments, or other external factors for your self-worth. To recognize your self-worth, remind yourself of what is stated in What Is Self-Worth & How Do We Build It? by Courtney E. Ackerman, MA.:

- You no longer need to please other people.

- No matter what people do or say, and regardless of what happens outside of you, you alone control how you feel about yourself.

- You have the power to respond to events and circumstances based on your internal sources, resources, and resourcefulness, which are the reflection of your true value.

- Your value comes from inside, from an internal measure you've set for yourself.

I want to remind you that regardless of what others say or how things may look, you matter, your feelings matter, your thoughts matter, your opinions matter, your mental health matters, your ambitions matter, and your peace matters. Stop comparing yourself to others because you don't have to. Have you ever tried walking in someone else's shoes that are not your size? It does not feel comfortable, does it? So why do we constantly compare ourselves to others? We do not know what their walk has been like.

In the biblical story of King David, his life looked unpromising. He was underestimated, undervalued, and hated by not only the giants, but his father-in-law as well. But guess what? David did not let this stop him because he knew God's promises over his life. David never gave up or in; he remained close to God and waited for him to act, and we know that when God acts, he shows out!

Despite David's pain, he knew that God could turn it around in his favor even when his life did not look good. Your life may not look like you think it is supposed to look, but I need you to get like David.

Sis, you have promise, value, and worth, so give yourself some compassion. What is your survival story?

Let's Reflect:

Do I value myself?

Do I believe that I am worthy of God's promises?

Do I extend myself grace?

How do I handle rejection?

What can I do to become the best version of myself?

I found this Self Esteem Checkup worksheet in an article by Courtney E. Ackerman, MA. What Is Self-Worth & How Do We Build It? (Incl... Worksheets). I would like you to take some time to complete this worksheet, as it will help you gain a better understanding, acceptance, respect, and love for yourself.

The worksheet lists 15 statements and instructs you to rate your belief in each one on a scale from 0 (not at all) to 10 (totally or completely). These statements are:

1. I believe in myself.
2. I am just as valuable as other people.
3. I would rather be me than someone else.
4. I am proud of my accomplishments.
5. I feel good when I get compliments.
6. I can handle criticism.
7. I am good at solving problems.

8. I love trying new things.

9. I respect myself.

10. I like the way I look.

11. I love myself even when others reject me.

12. I know my positive qualities.

13. I focus on my successes and not my failures.

14. I'm not afraid to make mistakes.

15. I am happy to be me.

Add up all the ratings for these 15 statements to get your total score, then rate your overall sense of self-esteem on a scale from 0 (I completely dislike who I am) to 10 (I completely like who I am). Finally, respond to the prompt, "What would need to change for you to move up one point on the rating scale? (i.e., for example, if you rated yourself a 6, what would need to happen for you to be at a 7?)."

Chapter 9

Purpose is Calling

Your purpose is hidden in your pain.

When troubles of any kind come your way, consider it an opportunity for great joy. For you know that when your faith is tested, your endurance has a chance to grow. So let it grow, for when your endurance is fully developed, you will be perfect and complete, needing nothing. James 1:2-4

Sis, you will experience some hardships, but it is in this pain that your faith matures. Jonah 4 shows us that the Samaritan woman at the well had been married five times, and Jesus did not count her out. Don't count yourself out or let others count you out because you have a complicated past. Jesus preserved your future for your purpose. Have you realized yet that struggle produces strength? You may feel like you are not educated, experienced, or connected enough because, truth be told, I did. God's word tells us in Proverbs that your gift will make room for you. Have you ever heard this statement? God does not call the qualified; he qualifies the called.

Well, it is so true. God will equip you for your purpose. Now, that does not mean you cannot get that extra education, training, or wisdom. But know that if God called you to it, he would see you through it!

It is time to heal, forgive, and let go of some things. Remember Joseph in Genesis 45:1-8? His brothers sold him, but it was because of God's grace that he was able to forgive them. Joseph told his brothers, once they realized who he was, not to be angry at themselves for selling him because God sent him there to preserve their lives and the lives of their families.

You see, God chose him for such an appointed time, he had a plan and purpose for Joseph, and although he had to endure some things, he fulfilled his purpose. Do you believe that your situation and hardships are too big for God? Do you believe that they were designed to destroy you? When in actuality, their purpose was to fulfill the greater plan that God has. Do not allow your hardships to define your life because God's story for you is not finished.

Memorize Jesus' words that were recorded in John 15:16 "You didn't choose me. I chose you. I appointed you to go and produce lasting fruit so that the Father will give you whatever you ask for, using my name." This means that his promises are ours, yours, and mine. Tap in when you feel unworthy, doubtful, anxious, impatient, burned out, unmotivated, underqualified, or overwhelmed. You are not a MISTAKE! Our Father said you were CHOSEN! If God chose you, who has the right to tell you any different? Romans 5:3-5 states, we can rejoice too, when we run into problems and trials, for we know that they help us develop endurance. And endurance develops character, and character strengthens our confident hope of salvation. And this hope will not lead to disappointment.

Sis, your purpose is hidden in your pain, and until you discover the purpose, it will remain painful. Have you ever stopped and asked yourself why you are experiencing the pain? Or have you tried to determine the source of it? God's word tells us that all things work together for our good, so that means that pain does, also. So, it is your choice to wallow in it or to use it to birth your purpose. Many of us miss the opportunity to walk in our purpose because we try to avoid the pain only to realize that it is inevitable. Pain will not destroy you, but it will reveal you to yourself!

Friends, let me let you in on a little something. At times we go through things that are not for us. It is meant for God to get the glory. We have an assignment, and, in that assignment, there are people attached to our lives, and they can only get to their purpose once we get to ours. Let that marinate a bit. Sometimes God must break your heart to save your soul. The reason brokenness is beautiful is because of how God can use it in our lives. It is something that can draw us near to Him. Brokenness can make room for a contrite heart and repentance to bring us back into fellowship with Him when we have failed.

Have you ever had a car needing repair or was in an accident and could not afford to take it to the dealership? Have you seen those recycled car part yards like Pull a Part or Pick n Pull? These yards contain various vehicles that have been wrecked or that have some malfunction, but although they are broken, they still have a purpose. They still have salvageable parts that can be stripped and placed on another vehicle to help that vehicle at its full potential. Ladies, Broken crayons still color! I used to be like a broken crayon because of my past and feeling unworthy until God showed me that just like a broken crayon still has a purpose, so do I.

Be done with letting your past control your future! Remember Eve? Yeah, you probably do from her most shameful mistake of eating that darn apple. Like Eve from the bible, not the rapper, many of us are remembered for our most shameful experiences, whether it is divorce, kids out of wedlock, infidelity, teenage pregnancy, etc. Our experiences may change our vision, confidence, and how we value ourselves, but they do not change God's. We still have PURPOSE! So, rise above fear, anxiety, insecurity, shame, depression, pride, and all the other barriers that consume your mind. Let's look at Mary. She was entrusted with the most important purpose, the birth of Jesus. However, it was also the most embarrassing position to be in because she was an engaged virgin who became pregnant. Yes, she was pregnant with Jesus, but did her family and friends believe her explanation that she had become pregnant through the work of the Holy Spirit? Why did God have to put Mary through such an embarrassing situation?

Listen, not everyone will understand what God is doing in your life, but I want you to stay encouraged. Chile, imagine the stares, passive-aggressive remarks, eye rolls, and judgment she received. I don't know about Yawl, but I would have been throwing some hands. You still have a purpose despite your brokenness, so evolve in it. God has given you power, purpose, and potential. You can breathe because you have been given lungs, oxygen, and an environment that sustains life. You have the ability to think, dream, plan, create, design, write, sing, dance, or do whatever you want to do because you have been given the desire, talent, gift, and ability to do so. Therefore, you have a purpose! Do not let the consequences of your actions keep you from reaching your purpose. Just because your situation changed does not mean God removed his purpose from your life. It is still within you, and you may have to learn to pivot. But know that your purpose will follow you because it is yours.

It is up to you to give birth to your purpose. When a mother gives birth, she produces a baby (a whole human) from her body, one of the most powerful things we can experience. There are three stages of labor. "During these three stages of labor, your body will prepare for the birth of your baby (stage one), deliver the baby (stage two), and deliver the placenta (stage three). Throughout labor, your body will contract to dilate and efface your cervix (Cleveland Clinic Medical, "Labor & Delivery: Signs, Progression & What to Expect"). When you go into labor, you will notice that the frequency, duration, and timing of your contractions will change. Right before you go into labor, most mothers begin nesting. Nesting is cleaning and organizing.

I am here to tell you that the pain, hurt, shame, anger, disappointment, embarrassment, and loneliness you are experiencing are your contractions. It is time you start cleaning and organizing your life to prepare to give birth to your purpose. Stop putting God in a box because he can use anyone. God CHOSE you and me, and in 1 Peter 4:10, he says, "Each of you should use whatever gift you have received to serve others as faithful stewards of God's grace in its various forms." Remember, God uses ordinary people like you and me to birth his purpose. Sis, your purpose is within you, and it is waiting to be released!

God, nothing compares to you! You alone are good, and you alone are majestic. You alone are praiseworthy!

Thank you for creating us, calling us by name, and giving us divine purpose. Lord, we trust you even when things seem like they are going haywire. We know that you cause things to die or decrease in our lives so that you can increase in our lives. Help us to see what you see in us and let everything that we do be pleasing to you and bring honor to your name. In Jesus' mighty name, Amen! Sis, when you hit blockages in your life, you are hitting opportunities. Our purpose gives us significance and growth, and it is what makes us rise every morning. Finding your purpose requires you to be honest with yourself, but once you uncover it, you will see a clearer vision and stop criticizing yourself. You are fearfully and wonderfully made. God took his time to mold you for a purpose; therefore, no door can close that he opens. I don't know about you, but it's God's best for me! Hello Sis, your purpose is calling. Will you answer?

I ran across this on Facebook and wanted to share it with you because it blessed me. I was in Dollar Tree last night, and a lady and her two kids were behind me in the LONG line. One was a big kid, and the other one was a toddler. The bigger one had a pack of glow sticks, and the toddler was screaming for them. The mom opened the pack and gave him one, which stopped his tears. He walked around with it smiling, but then the bigger boy took it, and the toddler started screaming again. Just as the mom was about to fuss, the older child bent the glow stick and handed it back to the toddler. As we walked outside, the toddler noticed it was glowing; and his brother said, "I had to break it so that you could get the full effect from it." I almost ran because I could hear God saying to me, "I had to break you to show you why I created you. You had to go through it so you could fulfill your purpose." Author unknown

Some people are content just "being," but you and I are CHOSEN, and we had to be broken. We had to get sick. We had to lose a job. We had to go through a divorce. We've had to bury our spouse, parents, best friend, or child. It was in those moments of desperation that we were broken. But…when the breaking is done, we will be able to see why we were created. Our GLOW just shows that we were once BROKEN!

P- assion/Poise

U-plift/Unity

R-esilence/Revolutionize

P-rayer/Powerful

O-bedience/Overcomer

S-olace/Successful

E-volve/Excellence

Let's Reflect:

Is my past controlling my future?

What worries me about my future?

Am I putting God in a box?

What is my assignment? Will I accept it?

What gives me the utmost fulfillment in life?

Chapter 10

Hello Love

"My biggest discovery was that you can literally re-create your life. You can redefine it. You do not have to live in the past. I found that not only did I have a fight in me, I had love." - Viola Davis

It took me quite some time before I began to desire a serious relationship again, but at the same time, I knew that I didn't want to be a lonely old lady. It was hard to trust because I assumed that men did not take me too seriously due to being a divorced mother of two, and all I would hear was that I was looking for a rebound relationship. So as my defense mechanism, I would only deal with you when I wanted to deal with you.

Getting back into the dating game was harder than I thought. I would meet men out and about, and I also tried a couple of dating apps, and this was such a mistake. If you think people have a hard time with people portraying themselves differently in person, try online dating. Through this process, I began to become more focused on the intentions of people and their actions. I saw this as a way of dissecting people's motives. I also noticed that people tend to put on a mask in the beginning because they are trying to win you over. I became more guarded, developed a lower tolerance for lying, and did not trust men as easily. Although I am happily married now, it took me some time because I had to learn to love myself before I could truly love someone else. I also had to realize that I was worthy of being loved.

My divorces and failed relationships did not feel good, but I needed those experiences to grow to appreciate what I had been blessed with. I was able to uncover aspects about myself that I may have never acknowledged. Ladies, I joked with my girlfriends the other night when we were having girl talk, saying that I had kissed many toads before I was awarded my King. I found myself in relationship after relationship and had to figure out the root cause. I had never taken the time to learn my needs, get to know me, or love myself. To fall in love with me. Truth be told, I had been in and out of so many relationships that I did not know how to be alone, and I found myself undervaluing myself for guys who did not deserve me. Like me, I am sure that many of you are also guilty of undervaluing yourselves. Stop undervaluing and undermanaging yourself because you seek companionship. Let me tell you something; men will pick on this and only give you what they think you deserve. The aura you put off lets them know they can get the bare minimum. Snap out of that comma and stop being that woman who will accept anything less than you deserve for the sake of not being alone. It is ok to be alone!

When God and life began to slow me down and prepare me for this first-time experience, I was completely lost. I did not know how to go to dinner by myself; it felt weird to see a movie alone. To me, it seemed awkward, embarrassing, sad, and a bit intimidating. I was just used to something else. I was always the one saying, "Girl, I could never do that," until I found myself doing just that, and I found it to be liberating at times. I had to change my mindset and start enjoying my alone time. I could enjoy myself without being irritated and meet new people if I chose to. I started learning how to enjoy my own company so much that I started taking myself on vacations.

Once I truly accepted and learned how to love myself, I discovered that I did not need anyone else's approval for love. It does not matter if you are falling in love with yourself for the first time or falling in love with yourself again. It is essential to your happiness. No one is responsible for your happiness but YOU! I am all about the self-love journey because many of us do not truly know ourselves, and self-love comes from knowing yourself. Think about this, as a child, your thoughts and values of yourself are shaped by your parents and loved ones. Then as you become older, those same thoughts are influenced by your experiences and other people. Before you know it, you are in your first relationship and have not taken the time to figure out who you really are and what you desire. When you have a strong sense of self-love, you understand your value, appreciate your strengths and weaknesses, and treat yourself in a loving way.

All of which spills over positively onto your mental well-being, interactions with people, and relationships. Self-love is important because it motivates positive behaviors and empowers us to keep pushing toward success in that career, passion, dream, and relationship. Without self-love, we self-sabotage because we do not know what deserves our energy and what does not. Why the self-sabotage? Because, at times, we struggle with the negative biases that stem from the lack of acceptance and shame we received as an adolescent.

Some suggestions for learning to love yourself:

- Go off the grid. Spend some alone time and learn what you like. Go to a movie or dinner. Enjoy a massage or take a nice hot bath. Go to the park and read a good book. Learn how to pray, meditate, and journal.

- Be kind to yourself. You do not have to look like a social media model to be worthy of love.

- Speak positively to yourself. It's ok as long as you don't talk back, lol. If you had a friend that spoke to you in the manner in which you speak to yourself, what would be the nature of your relationship? Remember, words have power, and negative talk could become a self-fulfilling prophecy.

- Practice Self Care. Creating habits like exercising and eating healthy can train your brain to think positively.

- Discover your purpose. This gives you a reason to get up in the morning and motivates you to keep striving for better.

- Give back. This was essential for me. It made me feel so good to help others in need. Giving back gives you a sense of purpose; it is the secret to loving yourself and showing love for others.

In Jeremiah 29:11, the Lord says, "For I know the plans I have for you. They are plans for good and not for disaster, to give you a future and hope." I finally learned how to sit and wait for God, but even then, I tried to pray him away. Girl, let me go ahead and tell you a secret, waiting on God is not always easy. In this age of women's empowerment and the business of life, we rarely have time to sit and wait for anything. But God sent me everything I prayed for, someone that I could communicate with, someone who loves me for me, someone who could pray for me and with me, someone that I could do life with, someone who would love my children and accept them as his own, someone that loves God, someone that is faithful, someone that I enjoy being around, someone that is supportive in me being my best self, someone that respects my time, someone that helps to motivate and encourage me, my lover, and protector.

I had known him for years. We met at the age of fourteen and dated in high school, but I still was not sure because I was scared at the thought that he could be my husband. The therapist stated that I kept looking for him to unmask because I was not used to being in healthy relationships. I thought it was because we were such good friends that I was scared to mess that up if it did not work out. Although we dated in high school, we broke up entering our senior year. I moved and changed schools, and we continued our lives. We had remained friends (without benefits) through college and adult life and kept in touch every few years. I had gotten married and had kids, as did he. We never interfered with each other's marriages or relationships and did not talk again until many years later. Fast forward to 2017, I had been in a relationship that I knew was not right for me, and I was praying my way through. I received a text message from my now husband, just saying hello and telling me that the kids and I had been on his mind and asking if he could pray for me. Of course, I was shocked, but I was like,"

Heck yes"! We prayed and stayed in contact as friends. I was able to walk away from that relationship, and my husband and I were married in December 2018. My husband loves me unconditionally, and he is everything that I did not know that I needed. He is #myforeverlove.

To wait on God, you must trust and give him complete control. When we take control, we end up with the wrong people, but God already knows who our husbands are. My husband tells me all the time that when he was a preteen, he asked God to send him his wife. Of course, not knowing when we met at the age of fourteen that I was what he had asked for. Surrendering your heart and desire for God is a posture that shows that you trust him to do his will for your life.

You need to know that you are too deserving of being loved and capable of loving. Do not rush and seek God! It's not a race; it is a marathon. Slow it down; although it's not a universally applicable rule, some individuals have experienced success in quick relationships. Taking your time or, as we say, baby steps in learning each other greatly benefits the relationship and may save you both some heartache.

As you prepare for your new adventure back into the dating game, be ready to make some mistakes, as no one is perfect. Be cautious but know that with patience, persistence, prayer, and clear objectives, you can find love again. Let me tell you something hilarious that my cousin told me. She told me that I was kicked out of the single pool and, therefore, I could not return. Ladies, can I tell you all that this is one pool I am elated to be kicked out of. I do not ever want to return to that pool, but I invite you beauties to keep swimming. But before diving in, ensure you are over your ex and know that chemistry is not always everything. Sometimes, it takes a while, and you have to come with a new mindset because things have changed since you were last in this pool.

Listen, ladies, some of you have this big old ridiculous list of what you want in a man. I know because I was once there. You see the list like, I want my man to be 6'7, dark and handsome, a body like the rock, driving a Bentley, a millionaire, a voice like Maxwell, and no kids - when you have four or five. Yeah, that list.

When creating your list of desired attributes in a potential husband, it is important to remember that it is not a strict rule. Instead, it can be helpful to relax, have fun, and trust God's plan. Sometimes, the person who is meant for you may not possess all the qualities on your list. Additionally, it is crucial to consider your own attributes while making this list. I am not saying that you should not have standards, but some of our standards can be ridiculous. Just because a man meets all that criteria and can afford to buy you the world does not mean they will respect you and treat you in a manner you should be treated as his lady. Financial success and stability are admirable, but let me tell you all how money is not always everything, and in all cases, it can't buy love. Remember my cousin, the one married to the narcissist? Well, she was very financially stable, as was her ex. Their combined income was slightly over half a million dollars a year, so money was never a problem. The mistreatment, power, and control within the marriage were. I am happy to tell you she is now living her life happy and unbothered because, in her darkness, she was able to find light. Her love story now is not as financially stable, but she has exactly what she prayed for and needs. God sent her a man that loves her unconditionally and treats her with the utmost respect.

Experiencing heartbreak can be devastating; it may seem impossible to love again after a divorce, and it may take some time because you invested years of trust, effort, and vulnerability. But if love is what you truly desire, do not give up on it. The love you give to others should be an overflow of the abundance of love you have for yourself. Find your happiness and love from within. Self-love is not just self-care. It is built of inner peace and happiness. Holding ourselves accountable and engaging with our feelings produces the strength and resilience necessary to embrace our emotions. Ask yourself, Am I ready to submit my heart, desires, and plans to God and wait on him?

Let's Reflect:

Have I allowed myself time?

Am I willing to settle for the fear of being alone?

Do I love myself, and am I ready to love someone else?

Does the dating process overwhelm me?

Do I believe that I am worthy of being loved?

Am I willing to submit?

Do I have healthy relationship boundaries?

What precautions will I take in the next relationship?

Afterword

Beautiful Brokenness will help you shift your mindset, gain clarity, and develop new coping mechanisms. Creating a healthy emotional and mental environment for yourself is essential. Surround yourself with supportive and loving people who uplift and encourage you. Seek professional help, if needed, such as therapy or counseling, to work through any unresolved issues and gain tools to cope with the emotional challenges you may be facing.

Remember that your past does not define your future. While divorce may have been a part of your journey, it does not limit your potential for happiness, love, and fulfillment. Embrace the opportunity to redefine your life and walk into the purpose you believe God has intended for you. Be patient with yourself as you heal and navigate this new chapter in your life. Healing takes time, and everyone's journey is different. I may have been wounded, but I was not destroyed. My WOUNDS have now become SCARS- a reminder that I am healed. Trust in your resilience and the strength that comes from your faith. Allow yourself to grow, learn, and embrace the possibilities that lie ahead.

Letting go of a relationship is an incredibly challenging and emotional experience to navigate, and understandably, you would seek support and guidance during this time. However, it's important to remember that the end of a relationship doesn't mean the end of your own life or happiness. In fact, it can be a transformative experience that allows you to discover your authentic self and ultimately live a more fulfilling life. I was able to let go after first acknowledging and accepting my emotions. It's natural to feel sadness, grief, anger, fear, insecurity, rejection, or even confusion when a relationship ends. Holding onto these emotions can hinder your ability to move forward, heal and find peace.

Acknowledge these emotions and allow yourself to feel them, but also work on letting them go and replacing them with more positive and empowering emotions. While it may be tempting to hold onto the memories and cling to the past, it's important to recognize that doing so will only prolong your healing and delay you in discovering your purpose.

During my difficult times, I tapped into my faith and sought solace in God as a source of comfort and strength. I utilized the tools and strategies mentioned to help me process my emotions and provide insight, perspectives, and practical advice on healing and rebuilding my life after divorce. I transformed my pain and challenges into lessons that have propelled me to grow and elevate myself. Taking responsibility for one's role in the dissolution of a marriage is a significant step toward healing and personal growth.

In addition, learning to co-parent and establish a successful parenting partnership is crucial for the well-being of your children. By prioritizing their needs and maintaining open communication with your co-parent, you can create a stable and supportive environment for them. Managing your finances through a realistic budget is another important aspect of rebuilding your life and ensuring stability for yourself and your family. It's important not to compare yourself to others or conform to their expectations because their story is not your story. Embrace your uniqueness and live your life authentically, honoring your values, dreams, and aspirations.

"Don't be afraid to start over. This time, you are not starting from scratch; you're starting from experience". ~Author unknown

Remember, you are deserving of love, compassion, and joy. Treat yourself with kindness and nurture your growth. Embrace the freedom that comes with releasing yourself from the emotional burden of the past. The journey of letting go may not be easy, but it can lead you to a place of self-discovery and personal growth.

Ultimately, your relationship with yourself is the foundation for your happiness and fulfillment. Finding your authentic self is a powerful way to reclaim your life and rediscover your worth. Take this time to reflect on your values, passions, and goals. Focus on self-care and engage in activities that bring you joy and fulfillment. Rediscover old hobbies or explore new ones. Spend time with loved ones who support and uplift you. Take care of your physical and mental well-being through exercise, meditation, journaling, or other practices that resonate with you.

Your resilience and dedication to self-improvement are truly commendable, and I wish you all the best on your continued path of healing and personal transformation.

Sis, remember that your purpose is hidden in your pain. God's love and grace have the power to mend our brokenness and bring about positive transformations.

As you continue your journey, remember to lean on your faith and trust in the process of restoration. Embrace the beauty that can arise from the broken pieces, knowing that God's presence and guidance are with you every step of the way. Now, GO change the trajectory of your story by discovering your purpose and living your next best life!

One day she discovered that she was fierce, strong, and full of fire and that she could not hold herself back because her passion burned brighter than her fears.
~ Mark Anthony

Life is not about waiting for the storms to pass. It's about learning how to dance in the rain. ~ Vivian Greene

Nothing can dim the light which shines from within. ~ Maya Angelou

Don't be afraid. Be focused. Be determined. Be hopeful. Be empowered. ~ Michelle Obama

About the Author

SHAKELA T. MATTHEWS is a newly inspired author from Atlanta, Georgia, passionate about uplifting women and helping them recognize their value and beauty. The daughter of Joe and Betty Whitehead Sr and wife to Gregory Matthews, she is also a mother, Air Force Airman, businesswoman, and real estate agent who expertly balances her career in the United States military, ministry, entrepreneurship, and family.

She is the virtual director for Chosen Women Empower, an organization dedicated to inspiring and empowering women from all walks of life. She enjoys baking, music, traveling, dancing, and having a good time!

References

Courtney E. Ackerman, MA. "What Is Self-Worth & How Do We Build It? (Incl.. Worksheets)." PositivePsychology.Com, 26 Apr. 2023, positivepsychology.com/self-worth/. (Chap 8)

"Financial Considerations in a Divorce: U.S. Bank." Financial Considerations in a Divorce | U.S. Bank, 19 Aug. 2021, www.usbank.com/wealth-management/financial-perspectives/financial-planning/financial-planning-for-divorce-dividing-money-after-split.html. (Chap 7)

"How to Clean up Your Money Mindset with Keina Newell." Wealth Over Now, 26 Jan. 2022, wealthovernow.com/how-to-clean-up-your-money-mindset/. (Chap 7)

"How to Deal with Rejection: 7 Tips." How to Deal With Rejection: 7 Tips, www.betterup.com/blog/how-to-deal-with-rejection. Accessed 1 June 2023. (Chap 8)

"How to Shift Your Money Mindset in 5 Easy Steps." Money Mentors, 5 Jan. 2023, moneymentors.ca/money-tips/how-to-shift-your-money-mindset/. (Chap 6)

Losson, Vicki, et al. "When Your Marriage Car Takes a Wrong Turn." Growthtrac Ministries, 22 Oct. 2020, www.marriagetrac.com/when-your-marriage-car-takes-a-wrong-turn/. (Chap 8)

Professional, Cleveland Clinic medical. "Labor & Delivery: Signs, Progression & What to Expect." Cleveland Clinic, 16 Feb. 2022, my.clevelandclinic.org/health/articles/9676-labor-delivery#:~:text=During%20the%20three%20stages%20of,dilate%20and%20efface%20your%20cervix. (Chap 9)

Taylor H, 2007, Sent to Heal. A handbook on Christian healing. Roseville, MN: Speedwell Press (Chap 4)